POCKET STUDY SKILLS

Kate Joseph and Chris Irons

MANAGING STRESS

D0100795

macmillan
international
HIGHER EDUCATION

palgrave

First published 2018 by
PALGRAVE

Palgrave in the UK is an imprint of Macmillan Publishers Limited,
registered in England, company number 785998, of 4 Crinan Street,
London, N1 9XW.

Palgrave® and Macmillan® are registered trademarks in the United States,
the United Kingdom, Europe and other countries.

ISBN 978–1–352–00177–8 paperback

This book is printed on paper suitable for recycling and made from fully
managed and sustained forest sources. Logging, pulping and manufacturing
processes are expected to conform to the environmental regulations of the
country of origin.

A catalogue record for this book is available from the British Library.

A catalog record for this book is available from the Library of Congress.

Contents

Acknowledgements

We would like to thank the many people who have helped us to produce this guide. The students we have worked with over the years at UCL and other universities have been the main inspiration. Their openness and courage in sharing their experiences of the ups and downs of university life has helped us to learn how to help them manage stress and other difficult feelings. Several students also commented on the book and we would like to thank them in particular.

University colleagues have also been instrumental in advising and supporting us: Barry Keane and Catherine McAteer (Managers at UCL Student Psychological Service), Richard Irons (Academic Registrar, University of Derby) and colleagues from the Compassionate Mind Foundation.

Thanks too to Sallie Godwin for her inventive illustrations and to Helen Caunce and Kate Williams at Palgrave for their guidance in making the project happen.

Finally, a thank you to Adam and Korina for their enthusiasm and encouragement.

Introduction

University is a time of change. It involves new academic and social experiences, and for many, new responsibilities, such as managing finances and fitting studies around work. The changes can trigger a range of feelings, from excitement and joy, to apprehension, anxiety, and loneliness – sometimes all at once! Transitions occur at different stages of university life, and any of these can contribute to feelings of stress.

Transitions at different stages of university

Transition at university	New challenges
School or college to first-year undergraduate studies	Meeting new people; moving out of home; adapting to a new learning environment with less support
First-year to second-year undergraduate	Adapting to a more advanced level of classes; higher expectations for written work; maintaining friendships
Second-year to final-year undergraduate	Managing the pressure of final exams and dissertations; applying for work or further study

Transition at university	New challenges
Undergraduate to Master's studies	Becoming a researcher; adapting to an intensive course and the jump from undergraduate to postgraduate teaching
Master's to PhD	Developing your own research idea; planning a long-term project; having a viva to defend your research

If you're reading this, it may be that you've been finding life at university difficult recently, or that someone thought it might be helpful for you or for someone you know. The five parts of this book will help you to understand what stress is, why you experience it, and crucially, what you can do to manage it.

This guide can help you to:

- learn about what stress is, and why we experience it
- understand what happens in the brain and body when you get stressed
- identify your stress and anxiety triggers
- learn new coping strategies to manage stress from two evidence-based approaches: Cognitive Behavioural Therapy and Compassion Focused Therapy
- plan your time to prevent stress from becoming overwhelming
- learn to look after yourself to manage the ups and downs of university life
- find out what other sources of help and support are on offer.

This guide can't help:

▶ with specific psychological or mental health issues (e.g. depression, Obsessive Compulsive Disorder, Attention Deficit Hyperactivity Disorder, Asperger's Syndrome, psychosis) that may require treatment from a trained professional

▶ if you are very distressed. If this is the case you should seek professional help through your GP or University Counselling Service

▶ if you are in crisis or need urgent support. If this is what you're experiencing, you can go to your GP or the Accident & Emergency Department in your local hospital (see also, Ideas for Further support, p. 98 for crisis helplines).

Many people find it hard to manage stress alone. So, if you feel you need more support or longer-term counselling or therapy, see Ideas for Further Support, for accredited therapy organisations, p. 98

There are some ideas in this book that you can act on today to reduce the impact of stress on your life at university. Some of the ideas will take longer to sink in and for you to practise. We'll support you as you move through the book, and make suggestions for how you can best learn to practise and apply the skills. Further reading and Internet resources are recommended throughout to help you make progress.

Thinking patterns and emotions linked to stress are covered in Parts 2 and 3, before we look at study–life balance and productive studying in Parts 4 and 5.

The first step to managing stress is to learn a bit about what it is, and how to recognise when you experience it. Sometimes stress symptoms are not obvious or they can build up gradually over time, so it is worth becoming more attuned to the signs that you are becoming stressed. This can help you to take steps to manage stress earlier, so that it doesn't become too overwhelming.

Stress is a commonly used word, but what does it actually mean? The word has its origins in the Latin word 'stingere', meaning 'to draw tight', so a simple definition is 'a feeling of pressure or tension'.

3   What is stress?

Stress arises in a situation where a person is unsure if they can cope with the demands being placed on them. We can experience stress in many different situations – from physically threatening experiences (e.g. a car crash), health problems, relationship break-ups or bereavements, to day-to-day experiences (e.g. managing a heavy workload or completing a project with a deadline).

Stress can manifest in very different ways, from physical tension or discomfort, palpitations, worry and anxiety, to feeling overwhelmed, demotivated, or even numb.

The stress response

There are two main physiological stress responses:

1 An acute stress response, known as the sympathetic adrenal medullary pathway, or SAM for short. Here, when a threat is encountered, your hypothalamus activates the adrenal glands, which in turn release adrenaline into the blood stream. These responses help the body to prepare for immediate action (e.g. fight or flight), and lead to:

- an increase in heart rate and blood pressure
- an increase in blood flow towards major muscles and the heart
- an increase in glucose production for energy
- an inhibition of tissue repair, the immune response and digestion (all essential for long-term survival, but not important to deal with an immediate threat).

Once you find a way to manage the situation that triggered stress, the physiological stress response described above switches off, and the body returns to equilibrium.

2 A prolonged or chronic response, which involves the hypothalamic-pituitary-adrenal (HPA) axis.

Here, if you are unable to find a way to solve the stressful situation, or the stressor naturally lasts for a long time, this can trigger a different physiological response involving the pituitary gland and, ultimately, the production of a hormone called cortisol. This helps to keep the body alert and ready for action, but can have some unpleasant and even harmful long-term consequences. We will return to this on p. 14.

Are you stressed?

Stress affects our brain and body. The following vicious cycle shows how stress can impact on thoughts, feelings, physical sensations, and behaviours:

Vicious cycle of stress when writing an essay

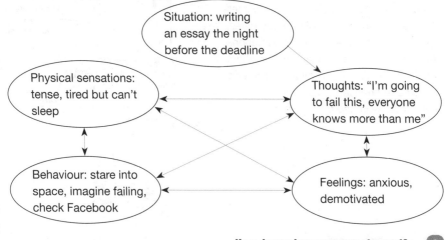

We experience the physical sensations of stress from head to toe – it can show itself in diverse ways, including headaches, spots, constipation, and palpitations (American Psychological Association, 2017). Sometimes you might not realise that you're stressed – you might instead feel numb, switched off or demotivated.

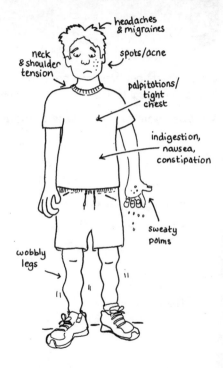

headaches & migraines

neck & shoulder tension

spots/acne

palpitations/ tight chest

indigestion, nausea, constipation

sweaty palms

wobbly legs

Your experience of stress in the past month

The following ten questions may help you to reflect on whether you are stressed, and how it might be impacting on your life. Reflect on your experience **over the past month**.

Circle 0, 1, 2, 3, or 4 to indicate how often you have felt a certain way.

0 = Never
1 = Rarely (e.g. once or twice a month)
2 = Sometimes (e.g. once or twice a week)
3 = Often (e.g. most days)
4 = All the time (e.g. every day)

1	How often have you felt stressed or anxious?	0 1 2 3 4
2	How often have you felt that you can't cope with your situation?	0 1 2 3 4
3	How often have you tried unsuccessfully to reduce your stress?	0 1 2 3 4

4	How often has being stressed stopped you from enjoying something (e.g. time with friends; a film or TV show)?	0 1 2 3 4
5	How often have there been so many worries on your mind that you don't know where to start?	0 1 2 3 4
6	How often has stress affected your sleep or appetite?	0 1 2 3 4
7	How often have you noticed physical signs of tension when you felt stressed (e.g. headaches, difficulties breathing, neck, shoulder or back tension, stomach problems)?	0 1 2 3 4
8	How often have you thought that the stress would never end?	0 1 2 3 4
9	How often has the stress affected your behaviour (e.g. either avoiding stress-inducing tasks or overworking to manage stress)?	0 1 2 3 4
10	How often have you worried about the fact that you get stressed?	0 1 2 3 4

Are you stressed?

- If you score mainly 0s and 1s, the likelihood is that you are not very stressed at the moment.
- If you score a combination of 1s, 2s, and 3s, you may be moderately stressed. It may be impacting on certain areas of your life.
- If you score mainly 3s and 4s, the chances are that you are feeling stressed at the moment and that it is impacting on your physical wellbeing and quality of life.

Your experience of stress can change from one day to the next, so don't worry too much about your scores. The good news is that this book suggests many ways to manage stress (see Parts 2 to 5).

Whilst short-term stress can be helpful and even healthy, chronic stress arises when stress is experienced over an extended period of time. This can happen when acute episodes of stress have been ignored or not properly managed. Chronic stress can have a variety of negative effects on our bodies, minds and, ultimately, our lives.

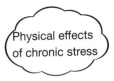

Physical effects of chronic stress

- insomnia
- tension headaches and migraines
- muscle pain
- increased risk of heart disease, Type 2 diabetes and stroke
- weakened immune system

- stomach ulcers or severe stomach pain
- reduced libido; erectile dysfunction, impotence; irregular or more painful periods

> Psychological and behavioural effects of chronic stress

- anxiety and inability to relax
- depression and demotivation
- burnout
- irritability and anger
- reduced social interaction or difficulties in relationships

- overeating or undereating
- drug and alcohol abuse
- difficulties making decisions and concentrating
- feeling overwhelmed

No, not at all. The acute and chronic stress responses are fundamental to our functioning and survival. In fact, at university some stress can help us to focus, to be energised and to get things done (e.g. playing sports and meeting deadlines).

Reflect Can you think of a situation when stress was helpful for you?

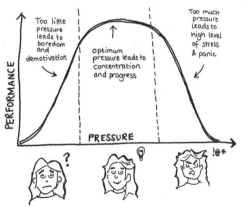

This graph shows how performance is reduced when there is either too little or too much pressure (Yerkes and Dodson, 1908).

Given that a moderate degree of stress can be motivating, how can we manage stress so that it does not become overwhelming?

The first step is to develop a different relationship with stress, so that stress becomes an ally, instead of an obstacle or enemy. As health psychologist Kelly McGonigal argues, it is not the amount of stressful experiences that determines a person's health and performance, but rather the person's perception of stress (McGonigal, 2015). This means that developing a healthier, more accepting relationship with stress actually changes your body's response to stress. Again, Parts 2 to 5 will explore how you can do this.

Although stress is a natural response that can be helpful in some situations, it can have negative impacts on health and performance. In Part 2, we look at how stress is triggered at university.

PART 2
STRESS TRIGGERS AT UNIVERSITY

Part 2 explores three key aspects of stress:

- What can cause stress at university
- How our minds contribute to our stress
- Mind training skills to manage stress, including mindfulness.

7 What are the common triggers of stress at university?

We can divide triggers into those that are external to us (i.e. that arise in the world around us), and those that are internal (i.e. that arise inside of us). Here are some examples:

External and internal stress triggers at university

External Triggers (things that happen outside of us)	Internal Triggers (things that happen inside our head)
Being away from home for the first time	Worrying that you won't cope without family and friends from home
Not having enough money to pay the rent	Worrying that you'll run out of money and get into lots of debt
Being told by your tutor that your work isn't good enough	Criticising yourself for not being good enough
Not being included on a night out with your flatmates	Ruminating about mistakes that you have made that caused you to be excluded

External triggers

There are common types of external stress at university. These include:

- Work, studying and exams
- Difficulties with friendships
- Difficulties with money
- Moving away from home

- Living with new people
- Being bullied, rejected or treated badly by others

Reflect What external stress triggers do you experience at university?

During your time at university it is inevitable that certain situations will cause you stress. Remember, in itself stress is not a bad thing. However, some of the external causes of stress can be managed practically to minimise their impact. Here are some ideas:

 Stress triggers at university

How to manage different forms of external stress

External stress	What helps?	Further information
Work, studying and exams	• Develop a timetable and plan for studying	For tips on study planning, look at the Pocket Study Skills books on *Time Management, Planning Your Essay* and *14 Days to Exam Success*.
Getting lower results than you expected	• Recognise that disappointments are part of life • Find out what you could have done to get a better grade (e.g. carefully re-read the feedback; speak to your tutor)	If there is something specific you want to learn to do differently, you could talk to your adviser or look at the relevant Pocket Study Skills books e.g. *Writing for University* or *Getting Critical*.
Difficulties with friendships	• Recognise that relationships can be tricky • Look at what might have contributed to the difficulties	If you're finding it difficult to navigate relationships, it might help to speak to someone at the university student support centre or university counselling service.

External stress	What helps?	Further information
Difficulties with money/finances	• Learn ways to budget and manage finances • Find a part-time job that provides some extra money but won't clash with your studies	Start with tips from the National Union of Students (NUS): www.nus.org.uk/en/advice/money-and-funding/money-management-tips/

Although it is worth trying to manage external triggers to stress, remember that many of the external stressors in the table above, like money and friendship issues, are simply part and parcel of life at university.

Internal triggers

One way to approach internal triggers is to first understand that the way our brain has been designed naturally contributes to stress. A simplified but useful way to understand this is to learn about the old and new parts of the brain. This is not complex neuroscience; it's some basic facts about how our brains have evolved, and how this can contribute to difficulties at university.

THEORY BOX: The old and new parts of the brain

Our old brain

It might seem strange, but parts of the human brain are hundreds of millions of years old. These brain structures originally evolved with the reptiles, and are associated with basic, primitive motivations sometimes referred to as the four 'f's: feeding, fighting, fleeing and ... having sex! Our old brain also contains structures that are key in motivating us (like they do in other mammals) to care for others and to be driven by status. These key motivations give rise to our basic emotions – anger, anxiety, sadness, disgust, and joy.

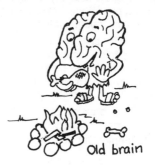

Old brain

Our new brain

Around two million years ago, our ancestors started to evolve along a line that led to a rapid expansion of 'new' brain areas (and in particular, the cortex and prefrontal cortex). These brain areas helped us to get smart – we developed sophisticated language skills, the ability to imagine things that aren't currently happening, the capacity to remember events from the past and predict what might happen in the future, and even to think about our thinking.

New brain abilities have led to great human achievements – works of literature and art, medicines and cures for illnesses, and a scientific understanding

New brain

of the universe. However, these same abilities to reflect on ourselves and the world can also backfire, creating loops in the mind that can trigger stress.

For more on brain structure and function, see *The Compassionate Mind* (Gilbert, 2009).

Example: Our new brain can keep us stressed

Imagine a zebra happily chewing away at the grass in the African savannah

… when it sees a lion creeping up on it

… the zebra gets scared and runs away (old brain)

… once it gets away from the lion, the zebra begins to calm down and goes back to happily eating grass again!

Let's change the example.

Imagine that you're walking back from a lecture, eating a tasty sandwich

… when you see a lion running towards you

… like the zebra, you get anxious and run away, and make it into your flat

… do you – like the zebra – calm down quickly and go back to enjoying your sandwich?!

… if not, why not? What 'new brain–old brain' loops in the mind do you have?

- What if it had caught me?
- What if it's still out there?
- What about my flatmates? They're still out there!

Rather than calming down like our friend the zebra, it's likely you'll remain on edge, stressed or dwelling on what happened. Now, whilst there aren't actually lions running around your university campus, there are various external and internal threats that can make you feel uneasy, anxious or upset.

How do our minds contribute to stress?

Common stress loops in the mind at university

Let's look at how these 'loops in the mind' can play out at university.

Dan is studying Law, and has just got an essay back with a disappointing grade. Although he enjoys his subject and has worked hard, in all three of the assignments he has submitted so far, he achieved lower grades than he expected. This triggered a series of responses – loops in the mind – for Dan:

Loops in the mind

New brain:

"Everyone gets it except me"

Old brain:

Anxiety

New brain:

"I'm going to fail my degree"

Old brain:

Heart racing, anxiety

New brain:

"I've let everyone down, I'm a loser"

Old brain:

Shame, low mood

Although it's not Dan's fault that he got caught up in these loops (of course, he, like the rest of us, did not choose to have the capacity to do this), it kept him in a stressed-out state for several days. It also made it harder for him to focus on his revision, which put him under greater stress.

Now that we can see how our minds naturally get caught up in tricky loops that can drive stress, it is time to think about what we can do about it. There are two steps to take:

i. Noticing loops in the mind
ii. Stepping out of loops

(i) Noticing loops in the mind

In order to deal with stressful old brain–new brain loops, the first step is to become aware of them. Just like it's helpful to notice that your ankle hurts after falling over and twisting it (so that you put ice on it and rest), you can apply the same approach to your mind.

Here are some helpful ways of learning to notice your mind loops:
▶ set a reminder on your phone to check in with what's happening in your mind
▶ put a reminder on a post-it note in your room or on your diary
▶ set a regular time to check in with your mind (e.g. breakfast, lunch and dinner).

Remember that all of us get into loops. It is just how the brain has evolved and if we start getting into a tussle with them (e.g. having thoughts like '*I shouldn't be struggling with these types of worries*'), then it tends to make things more stressful.

 Reflect Make a few notes about the thinking-feeling loops that cause you stress: (1) the trigger, (2) your thoughts, and (3) your feelings. Or set an intention to keep an eye out for them and then write them down when they come up over the next week.

(ii) Stepping out of loops

What can you do about the loops in your mind? It can help to direct your attention elsewhere. This can involve changing what you're doing, and trying to focus on something else (e.g. reading a novel, speaking to a friend).

These types of distractions can be helpful in the short term, but sometimes can lead to problems (see Part 5). You might also spend some time practising mindfulness.

Introducing mindfulness

Mindfulness is a powerful approach to managing loops in the mind – and for helping us to manage stress more generally. There are lots of different ways of describing mindfulness, but at its heart, it involves paying attention to the present moment without getting caught up in judgements, worries and rumination. You don't have to be religious or spiritual to practise mindfulness. Mindfulness involves exercises that all of us can benefit from.

Practising mindfulness is associated with:
- lower levels of stress, anxiety and depression
- improved immune system functioning
- improved sleep
- improved social connections and relationships.

The benefits of mindfulness above are from evidence-based research (see Useful sources, p. 104).

Mindfulness can help you to slow down and notice stress-based loops in the mind, and then practise grounding your attention in the present moment. If you are focusing on your breathing or sounds around you, or on what you are eating, it means that you are stepping out of the loops in your mind, and your attention is resting on something neutral or positive, rather than with stress-inducing thinking–feeling loops.

Managing the stressful thinking–feeling loops is a bit like building up a muscle in the body. If you want to develop stronger biceps, what is the best way? Most gym trainers advise a regular weight-training programme to build up muscles gradually. The same idea applies to managing stress. In fact, we could think of this as 'mind gym'! With practice, it is possible to build up the brain pathways that allow us to be more present in the here-and-now, and step back from common worries and ruminations.

Practising Mindfulness

A key point to hold in mind is that mindfulness does not have a specific 'result', like holding your attention in one place. The idea is to develop the skill of knowing where your mind is at any moment – a type of *mind awareness*. So the more your mind wanders and the more you notice it wandering, the more mindful you are! Here are some guidelines for a three-minute breathing practice.

EXERCISE: Three-minute breathing space

Take your time working through the following steps:
Find a place to sit in an upright but comfortable position.

1 If you can, close your eyes, or else pick a point to focus on in front of you.
2 Direct your attention towards your breathing. Begin to notice the sensation of breathing in and out.
3 Some people find it helpful to focus their attention on the area around the tip of their nose, noticing the sensation of air as it moves in and out. Or focus at the centre of the chest, noticing sensations as the chest expands on the in breath, and contracts on the out breath.
4 When other thoughts pop into your mind (maybe about what you're doing, e.g. 'this is boring' or 'I can't do this', or about what you need to do later in the day), just notice that your attention has drifted, and gently bring it back to your breathing.
5 Continue to notice the sensation of the in breath and the out breath, as if you were just observing this with curiosity.

Continue this process for around three minutes, gently noticing your attention and the sensation of breathing in and out. Remember that your breath can always be the anchor of your attention, something that you can always bring your mind back to, again and again.

If you are new to mindfulness, it is useful to have an audio track to guide you. A website like Mindfulness for Students (see Useful Sources) provides links to guided practices. There are also lots of apps that can help you to practise mindfulness (e.g. Headspace or Breathing Zone, see Useful Sources, p. 104).

Mindfulness in everyday life

You don't need to have a formal, meditation-like practice to develop your skills in mindfulness. We can all practise this as we're going about our daily routine. For example, the next time you have a shower, you could do this mindlessly (e.g. worrying about the seminar coming up, or how many things you've got to do) or mindfully – noticing the feel and warmth of the water against your skin, the smell of the shower gel or shampoo, or the sound of the water as it falls against the bath or shower tray.

Try this short exercise that you could practise right now. All you need is some food! It doesn't matter what kind of food you choose – it could be a strawberry, a sandwich, or a piece of chocolate.

EXERCISE: Mindful eating

1 Spend a few moments looking at the food in front of you.
2 Pick up the food and turn it around in your fingers. Notice its shape, texture and colour. Pay really close attention to each of these qualities.
3 Whilst noticing the sensations in your arm, slowly move the food up to your nose. Taking your time, pay attention to the smell.
4 Now taste the food – notice the different sensations of taste as you slowly chew the food, moving it around your mouth.
5 When you have finished chewing, notice how it feels to swallow the food.
6 Continue this process of mindful eating, and notice the difference between bites.

When you have finished mindful eating, reflect on what you noticed and whether this experience felt any different from your usual experience of eating.

See how you get on with the different ways of practising mindfulness. Remember, it's like anything you do in life: if you want to become good at the guitar or learn a new language, practice leads to progress. It's the same with mindfulness – you need to practise it like any other skill. Over time, you'll notice that you become more able to notice when you're caught up in a loop, and crucially, more able to step out of these loops and bring your mind back into the present moment.

We all get stressed from time to time, because the way our brains are structured contributes to stress. It can help to notice loops in the mind and learn how to step out of them (e.g. mindfulness). Part 3 moves on to look at how you can balance stress and other emotions.

STRESS AND EMOTION

Part 2 looked at how it is common to get caught up in thinking–feeling loops that contribute to stress. Part 3 explores how stress is linked to emotions and motives, and how balancing our emotions can help to deal with stress.

This may sound like a strange question, but it is worth asking why we have emotions in the first place. Given that our emotions can cause us pain and distress, why do we experience them? Let's take the example of physical pain. If you touch a hot pan and burn your finger, you feel pain – but what is the pain for? One function of pain is that it signals to you to be cautious, so as not to cause yourself damage.

Emotional feelings are similar in some ways to physical pain, in that they signal something. The sensation of pain evolved to remind us to stay away from things that could be harmful or dangerous, or to take care of our body if we have damaged it. Emotions like anger, sadness and anxiety are communications that can help us to understand what is happening in life and guide us on how to respond.

Let's see how this works for three emotions:

The functions of three common emotions

Emotion	Function	Example situation
Anxiety	Alerts us to potential threats and motivates us to defend ourselves (e.g. to avoid the threat)	Dana is feeling anxious that she won't be able to manage the demands of her new Master's course whilst also looking after her two young children.
Sadness	Alerts us to the loss of something important and signals the need for connection or support	Ruma is feeling sad and lonely during the first week of university, as she misses her family.
Anger	Alerts us to our needs being blocked in some way, or that we have been treated unfairly	James is feeling angry after his flatmate broke his laptop without apologising.

10 The Three System Model of Emotion

The Three System Model explains how emotions have evolved to serve different functions in our lives (Gilbert, 2009). It is based on evolutionary theory, neuroscience, and neurophysiological findings.

The three major emotion systems are referred to as Threat, Drive and Soothing:

1 **The threat system**, with emotions of anger, fear and disgust, evolved to help us identify and respond to threats in the world.
2 **The drive system**, linked to emotions of excitement and joy, motivates us to move towards resources and goals that might be helpful to us.
3 **The soothing system**, linked to feelings like contentment, calmness and safeness, helps us rest and feel peaceful when we are not threatened or trying to achieve things. This system also motivates us to give and receive care from others. It can be a powerful way to balance out and regulate the impact of the other two systems.

Let's consider how this model relates to stress at university.

Stress and the threat system

There are many overlaps between stress and the threat system. The threat system evolved to detect threats in the world, and then motivate us to get safe and protect ourselves and others. It is linked to various stress responses in our bodies (as described in Part 1). When activated, the threat system directs different aspects of our minds.

You can see how this works in the diagram above.

The threat system can shape the mind and feelings in many ways.

Although it is understandable to feel nervous about an upcoming exam, unfortunately the threat system can sometimes fire too powerfully or too frequently, and this can prevent us from thinking clearly and from concentrating on what we need to do.

Example: How the threat system captures attention

It is the first week of university and you go to the hall bar. You talk to nine students, who all seem friendly, fun and interesting. However, one girl you meet looks you up and down, and then whispers to her friend before walking off. That night, your brother calls you to find out how the night went.

Which experiences do you tell him about? The nine positive ones or one unpleasant one? The chances are that you focus more on the girl who ignored you than the others who were friendly. If you tend to focus on the negatives, you are not alone. This happens because our brains are wired to look out for threats, so that we can find ways to deal with them and protect ourselves.

---

 think about how the threat system affects you. These questions may help:

- How often is your threat system triggered at university?
- What situations, experiences, thoughts or memories tend to trigger it?

- What type of threat emotions (e.g. anger, anxiety, shame) tend to get triggered in stressful situations?
- How do you behave when this system is triggered (e.g. aggression, flight, avoidance, submissiveness)?
- What happens to your thinking when this system is triggered? What type of thoughts do you have (e.g. worrying, ruminating, imagining)?

Stress and the drive system

Although managing threats is a concern for all animals, there is of course more to life than this. Animals also have to be motivated to pursue beneficial resources, and we are exactly the same! In order to pursue and get things in life, the emotions of the drive system – for example, anticipation and excitement – activate and energise us. When we are successful in getting the thing we targeted, this system can leave us with bursts of positive feelings such as excitement, joy, exhilaration, and elation.

The drive system is a great source of energy at university – motivating us to study, get good grades, and seek out social relationships. However, it can be related to stress when we feel blocked from achieving these goals in some way. Here is an example:

Example: Stress and blocked drive system

During his undergraduate course, Taj had found it easy to achieve good grades. He found essays and exams straightforward, and received one of the top grades in his year. However, since starting his PhD, he found studying alone harder than he had expected. Although he got on quite well with his supervisor, the lack of regular assignments meant he had no clear way to monitor his progress. His confidence from undergraduate days started to drop, and he believed that other PhD students in his year were way ahead of him. As this pattern continued through the year, Taj noticed he was dreading coming in to university, and became increasingly stressed and anxious about his work.

For Taj, not being given regular feedback on his performance (reduction of drive system activation) started to heat up his threat system (with thoughts like *'I'm not good enough'*). In turn, he began to feel demotivated (more loss of drive system), and did not get any satisfaction from progressing with his research. It can be common for threat and drive systems to interact in a way that also feeds our experience of stress.

Reflect How does the drive system work for you?

- How often is your drive system triggered at university?
- What situations, experiences, thoughts or memories tend to trigger it?
- What drive emotions do you experience in these situations (e.g. excitement, joy, happiness)?
- How do you behave when this system is triggered (e.g. pursuing, consuming, celebrating)?

- Does anything block you from experiencing your drive system at university?
- Do blocks to your drive system increase activation of your threat system?

Stress and the soothing system

When animals are not in a threat or drive state, it is important for them to slow down and experience periods of rest and recuperation. For humans, this can involve feelings of calmness, soothing, and contentment, and are linked to activation of the parasympathetic nervous system (the branch of our autonomic nervous system that is sometimes referred to as the 'brake' that naturally slows down and calms the threat–stress response). The feelings of the soothing system can also be triggered by experiences of care, kindness and support from other people. If rest or support is lacking, this can lead to stress, as in this example.

Example: Stress and the blocked soothing system

Chun came from a large, supportive family in a small town in China, where she had a close group of friends. She enjoyed her undergraduate degree in Shanghai and was excited to move to London to study for a Master's in Business Studies. However, when Chun arrived she began to experience a lot of stress adjusting to a new country

---

and culture, in a university where the teaching style and expectations for assignments were very different from home. The students in her flat were mainly Spanish and talked amongst themselves. Although she regularly phoned home and Skyped her old friends, it just didn't feel the same as when she was with them back at home, face-to-face.

Chun could not relax, as her soothing system was blocked. She began to realise that much of the stress was because she didn't feel cared for or close to anyone at university, and didn't feel she could get help and support to manage her struggles.

So the absence of the soothing system – particularly if we have been used to having supportive and caring people nearby – can actually be a source of increased stress at university. It can be difficult to develop new friendships and share difficult feelings, and for some, this leads to feelings of loneliness and of missing life back at home.

Reflect Think about how the soothing system works for you.

- How often is your soothing system triggered at university?
- What situations, experiences, thoughts or memories tend to trigger it?
- How do you behave when this system is triggered (e.g. reflecting, sharing feelings, being able to rest and slow down)?
- Does anything block you from experiencing your soothing system?

How are your three systems balanced?

Reflect Reflect on how your three systems are balanced, particularly in terms of stress at university:

- Is one system triggered more frequently or powerfully than the others?
- Are any of the systems not experienced very often?
- Try drawing out the three systems on a piece of paper so that the size of each circle represents how much you are experiencing each system at the moment. How big would each one be?

Managing stress by balancing the systems

How to reduce your threat system

Many of the 'loops in the mind', covered in Part 2, are actually threat-based loops. Mindfulness is one way to manage threat, and more strategies are introduced in Parts 4 and 5. For now, it's helpful to notice when your threat system is activated and how building up the drive and soothing system may help.

How to develop your drive system

Sometimes our threat systems are overactive at university because they take our focus and energy away from engaging in things that bring us pleasure and a sense of accomplishment. With this in mind, have a think about the following questions:

- Are there things that you used to enjoy doing that you do less of now?
- What activities could you do more regularly that might bring you a sense of pleasure, excitement, or accomplishment?

We will return to this in more detail in Part 4, p. 66

How to develop your soothing system

There are many ways to help our bodies and minds slow down so that we experience a sense of feeling calm and soothed. For practical ways to include more rest in your week, see Part 4, p. 68.

Imagery has a powerful impact on our feelings. If you bring an image to mind of a time in your life when you felt very anxious or angry, you'll probably begin to experience some of those feelings again. Similarly, if you bring to mind an image of the happiest or most intensely joyful moment of your life, then you're likely to have a flutter of those feelings. With this in mind, we can spend time purposefully developing images to build up the soothing system, as this helps to reduce stress levels.

Here is a brief imagery exercise that is designed to activate the soothing system.

EXERCISE: Creating an image of a calm, soothing or safe place

Find somewhere comfortable to sit where you will not be disturbed.

1 Breathe in and out in a soothing rhythm, allowing your breathing and body to slow down a little.
2 Spend some time bringing to mind an image of a place that you feel is safe, soothing or calming. This may be somewhere you have been before or somewhere completely 'made up'.

---

3 When an image has come to mind, spend a few moments exploring it with your senses. To start with, mindfully pay attention (around 30 seconds for each sense) to:

- what you can see in this image of your safe place. This might be colours, shapes, or objects.
- any sounds that are present in this image. Notice the different qualities the sounds have and how they make you feel.
- any soothing or comforting smells that are present in your image.
- physical sensations you can feel or touch, such as the warmth of the sun against your skin, or how the grass or sand feels beneath your feet.

4 Consider whether you are in your safe place on your own, or whether someone, or something else like an animal, is there with you.

5 As this is your own safe place, imagine that it has an awareness of you. It welcomes you there, and is happy to see you. It wants you to feel safe and calm. Notice how you feel knowing that this place wants you to feel supported, safe and at ease. Spend a minute or so just focusing on this.

Remember that you can bring this image of your safe place to mind whenever you want to feel calm or soothed.

Managing stress involves balancing emotion systems and you can do this with breathing and imagery techniques. Part 4 offers more ways to manage stress, such as small lifestyle changes that can make a big difference.

PART 4

LIVE WELL, STUDY WELL

Part 3 looked at how to find balance with our emotions, and Part 4 continues on the theme of balance to explore how lifestyle changes can help us to manage stress, and have more fun! Living well involves:

– Balance
– Looking after yourself
– Fun and rest.

12 Balance

It can be challenging to strike a healthy balance between work, rest, and play. Think about all the things you need to balance at university: cooking, cleaning, getting enough sleep and rest, attending lectures, doing coursework and exams, budgeting, friendships, and having fun … You may also have other things to manage, like paid work or caring for family members. Just reading these lists could be stressful in itself! Juggling the different aspects of university life isn't easy, so learning how to find balance can help to manage stress.

Even if you have a busy schedule and are juggling several responsibilities, you can find more balance by making lifestyle changes to make sure you look after yourself and include both fun and rest in your week.

Many people are good at helping others, and giving advice on how to be healthy. Unfortunately, we're often not so good at advising ourselves! The idea of self-care, of self-compassion (being sensitive to our own distress, and finding ways to try and do something helpful with this) might sound a little odd, but there are many ways we can focus on this (see Irons and Beaumont, 2017, for more information). For example, there are lots of small changes that you can make to look after yourself and manage stress effectively, such as changes to sleep, exercise, eating and drinking.

It is even more challenging to make time to look after yourself when you are studying and you also have other people to look after (such as children, elderly relatives or a friend in crisis). However, remember that you will be much better able to care for others if you feel well yourself. The idea is the same as on aircraft flights, where the advice is to fit your own oxygen mask before you try to help someone else.

Sleep

Prioritising getting enough sleep when you feel pushed for time can feel like an undeserved luxury. Some people find the idea of getting enough sleep is stressful in itself, as they could use the extra hours to study instead! However, sleep is essential for physical and emotional wellbeing, and for managing stress levels in a helpful way.

The quantity and quality of sleep impacts on concentration, memory, brain and heart health, productivity and even weight. Although it may feel like you are 'shutting down' when you go to sleep, your body is actually taking the opportunity to rest and restore vital bodily functions, such as your immune system, nervous system and muscles. In contrast, a regular lack of sleep can cause a variety of physical and psychological difficulties, and make us less resilient to coping with stress.

Here are some common myths about sleep.

Sleep: Myths and Reality

Myth	Reality
Getting one hour less sleep per night won't affect your daytime functioning.	Although you may not notice significant differences, regularly losing even one hour of sleep can affect your ability to think clearly and respond quickly. It can also compromise cardiovascular health, energy balance, and ability to fight infections.

Myth	Reality
Your body adjusts quickly to different sleep schedules.	Most people can reset their biological clock, but only by one or two hours per day at best. It can take more than a week to adjust after studying all night or travelling across time zones.
You can make up for lost sleep by sleeping more at the weekends.	Although this pattern may help you catch up on sleep, it will not completely make up for it. In fact, sleeping more at weekends can disrupt your sleep–wake cycle, and make it much harder to go to sleep at the right time on Sunday night.

(adapted from the National Institutes of Health, 2017)

The link between sleep, wellbeing and studying

Poor sleep quality has been linked to increased stress, poorer physical and psychological health, and decreased academic performance. A study of over 500 students found that the more they sacrificed sleep to study, the harder they found it to understand material and perform on tasks the next day (Gillen-O'Neel et al., 2013). Brain studies also show that sleep deprivation worsens working memory. So, if you stay up when you need to sleep, you could be reducing your capacity to remember what you have been learning (Chee and Chuah, 2008).

How much sleep do you need?

Adolescents and adults need around 7 to 9 hours' sleep a night. However, between 50% and 70% of students are not getting enough sleep (Hershner and Chervin, 2014). It might be okay for some people to sleep a little less or more than 7 to 9 hours, and certain circumstances may limit the amount of sleep you get (e.g. deadlines, child-care, shift work). However, it is worth trying to get into a regular pattern of at least 7 hours' sleep per night. There is a difference between the amount of sleep that allows you to get by and the amount of sleep that allows you to function at your optimum potential. Although many people think that they can manage on far less than 7 hours' sleep, over time this can lead to chronic sleep deprivation.

Whilst the quantity of sleep is important, so is the quality. Good quality sleep is characterised by the following factors (National Sleep Foundation, 2017):

- sleeping in bed for at least 85% of your total sleep time
- falling asleep after 30 minutes or less
- waking up no more than once per night, for no more than 20 minutes.

Many things can compromise our sleep quality, including irregular sleep patterns, caffeine and alcohol use, stress, and looking at screens before sleeping.

Tips for improving your sleep

- ▸ Try to set a regular time for going to sleep and waking each day.
- ▸ Don't drink caffeine or smoke before you go to sleep – in fact if you're sensitive to caffeine, don't have caffeinated drinks (e.g. tea, coffee, some soft drinks) after 5 pm.
- ▸ Have a technology or screen-free zone (especially smartphone/tablet/laptop) in the hour leading up to trying to sleep.
- ▸ Try not to check the time if you can't sleep, as this can cause more stress.

- If you can't sleep, rather than tossing and turning, it can help to get out of bed for a short while (e.g. to get a glass of water) before returning to try again.
- Develop your own pre-sleep routine to get you into a relaxed mood ready for sleep. Some ideas include having a shower or bath, reading a book that is not too stimulating, or listening to relaxing music.

Exercise

Students spend a lot of time in one place, often in their room or at a desk (e.g. during revision or before a deadline). Humans have evolved to be mobile and active – our bodies were not designed to sit still on chairs for long periods of time.

The link between exercise, wellbeing and studying

Exercise has important benefits for mood and stress. Doctors recommend around 2½ hours of moderate aerobic exercise per week (e.g. fast walking, cycling or swimming) as well as anaerobic exercise twice a week (e.g. short-duration, high intensity exercises that tone muscles, like weight training, or sit-ups). Exercise is so effective for managing mood fluctuations that GPs in the UK prescribe exercise for people with mild-to-moderate depression (NHS, 2016).

Don't worry if you don't like running or team sports – there are many options to try at university, from dance, yoga, trampolining and martial arts, to outdoor activities like hiking, sailing, and rock climbing. Or if you are pushed for time, try the 7-minute workout, a free app you can try at home with no equipment, that guides you through 12 different exercises (see Useful Sources, p. 104).

Regular exercise can also enhance your ability to study, as it contributes to improved attention, concentration, and processing speed (Points Sports Health, 2017). Aerobic exercise in particular has been found to boost the size of the hippocampus in the brain, which is linked to learning and memory (Godman, 2014).

Tips to start exercising

- If you are not used to exercise, start gradually with around 10 minutes a day.
- Find a form of exercise that you enjoy – you are much more likely to keep it up!
- Fit exercise into your daily routine. Get off the bus one stop early and walk the rest. Try using the stairs rather than taking the lift.
- Try a group class or join a university sports club – it could be a good way of getting fit and meeting new people.
- Commit to regular walks or jogs with a friend to motivate each other.
- Sign up to a 5km or 10km run so that you have a goal to train towards.

Eating

It makes sense that the fuel that we put into our bodies affects how we function and how we feel. Think about a car. If you try to run a car on too little fuel or on the wrong type (e.g. petrol in a diesel car), it won't be long before it breaks down. So, it is worth considering how you are 'fuelling' yourself to study.

"You are what you eat"

Although for some people acute stress can inhibit appetite, chronic stress can increase appetite and desire for certain types of food that taste nice (e.g. chocolate and sweets) but are not very healthy! Stress eating can involve:

- Eating more, which can be due to hormonal changes during ongoing stress that make us feel more hungry. Overeating can also be a way to block out uncomfortable feelings.
- Eating highly calorific, sweet or fatty foods that reduce stress through creating pleasurable feelings (Sominsky and Spencer, 2014).

Whilst it is understandable that people turn to tasty foods when they are stressed, becoming reliant on food as a way of managing stress can lead to vicious cycles of further stress, shame and self-criticism, and longer-term consequences such as weight gain and heart problems. Understanding how and why stress eating happens is helpful in order to develop healthier ways to manage stress.

Try to eat a balanced diet, which includes a mixture of fruit and vegetables, protein, carbohydrates and some fat. (See 'The Eatwell Guide'; Public Health England, 2016.)

Fruit and vegetables – the NHS recommends eating at least five portions of fruit and vegetables a day as part of a healthy diet, as they are a good source of vitamins, minerals and fibre. You can choose from fresh, tinned or frozen versions or fresh juice.

Tips for an affordable 5 a day

- Go for items that are in season as they are usually cheaper.
- Swap chocolate for a banana – they are full of energy and vitamins and cost less.
- Don't worry if fruit or vegetables are about to go out of date – you can use them to make a smoothie, stew or pasta sauce.

Carbohydrates (e.g. bread, rice, pasta, potatoes) are a vital part of a balanced diet, as they provide energy to concentrate. Some people cut out carbohydrates to lose weight, but it is important to make sure you include them to fuel your brain. Wholegrain carbohydrates are recommended as they release energy more gradually (e.g. brown rice and pasta, or leaving the skin on potatoes).

Protein is good for strength and helps the body build and repair. It can come from meat, fish, or non-meat options including eggs, tofu, beans, pulses, and lentils.

Dairy (e.g. milk, cheese, yoghurt) is important for bones. There are non-dairy alternatives that also contain calcium, such as milk made from soya, oats or rice.

Fat – contrary to popular opinion, not all fat is bad! Unsaturated fats are healthy sources of fat that are found in natural products like nuts and avocados. Although enjoying a treat like a packet of crisps is fine from time to time, try to limit the amount of processed foods you eat. Snacks that are high in saturated fats (e.g. crisps, biscuits and cakes) are tempting as they boost energy levels. However, this boost tends to be short-lived and is often followed by an energy slump, characterised by fatigue and hunger.

Tips for healthy eating

- Aim to have some carbohydrates or protein for breakfast to give you energy to start the day, and try to include a variety of food types during your meals.
- Have something to eat every three to four hours to keep your energy levels stable.
- If you get the urge to eat certain foods to cope with stress, try to 'surf the urge' by sitting with the feelings and letting them pass.
- Try to delay the urge to eat when you are stressed, by doing something you can't do whilst eating at the same time (e.g. have a shower, go for a walk, practise mindfulness).
- Keep hydrated throughout the day so that you don't mistake thirst for hunger (see next section on Drinking, p. 63).
- Don't eat at your desk – find somewhere to take a break and enjoy the food!

If you constantly feel tired or have been struggling to focus for some time, it may be worth seeing a doctor to have a blood test to check if there are any medical causes.

Drinking

As well as finding balance in what you eat, think about how you balance drinks including water, caffeine and alcohol.

Water

We need water to absorb vitamins and minerals, digest food, and allow the liver and kidneys to get rid of waste. How much water do you drink each day?

The UK government recommends drinking 6 to 8 glasses of water a day (around 1.2 litres in total) to keep hydrated. However, most people do not drink enough water; one study in 2013 found that up to 75% of adults were chronically dehydrated (Lee, 2013). The effects of dehydration can be headaches, feeling weak, and overeating (as sometimes we mistake thirst for hunger). All of these factors can contribute to stress.

8 glasses? easy...

Caffeine

It can be tempting to drink tea, coffee and energy drinks to stay alert. However, too much caffeine can lead to dehydration, agitation, and difficulties concentrating. Since everyone is different, try to get to know your body. Figure out when caffeine is giving you a much-needed boost and when it is actually reducing your productivity.

Alcohol

Alcohol is a part of many students' social lives. If you drink alcohol at university, it is worth understanding the impact alcohol can have on health, both in the short- and long-term.

In the short-term, having a hangover after excessive drinking impairs abilities on cognitive tasks (Verster et al., 2013). Although some people find that alcohol helps them to get to sleep, the effect wears off during the later stage of sleep. Moreover, it has been found to disrupt a phase of sleep known as REM – Rapid Eye Movement. Since REM sleep is important for consolidating memories, drinking alcohol can impair the storage of information from the day (Park et al., 2004). Excessive and chronic drinking can have negative impacts on the brain, nervous system, heart, liver and pancreas, and can lead to a higher risk of heart attacks and stroke (NHS, 2015).

So, think about your drinking and consider cutting down on regular drinking or stopping during stressful times, like the exam season. It is also worth reflecting on why you're drinking alcohol. It's common for students to drink alcohol when they're feeling good and want to have fun. However, like stress eating, alcohol can also be used to cope with stress and other unpleasant feelings. Unfortunately, drinking to manage stress can lead to mood changes, financial problems and difficulties with relationships.

Tips for balanced drinking

- Stay hydrated throughout the day, drinking water at regular intervals.
- Be mindful of how caffeine influences your concentration and sleep.
- Reflect on how and when you drink alcohol, and whether it is causing you any problems.
- Be aware that the NHS guidelines recommend no more than 14 units of alcohol per week for both men and women. This corresponds to around 6 pints of beer or 7 175ml glasses of wine for the whole week.

In Part 3 we introduced the Three System Model of Emotion. It is time to look at how to develop the drive system (linked to excitement and pleasure) and the soothing system (linked to resting and slowing down).

Fun

Although studying is important and it takes up a lot of time, don't forget to enjoy yourself! Doing what you enjoy helps to develop interests, meet new people, and may clarify what is important in your life. Crucially, fun is also a great antidote for stress.

What do you enjoy doing? When do you feel energised? What do you look forward to in the future? There is no right way to have fun; it is about trying out different activities to discover what 'floats your boat'. People get pleasure from a vast range of activities:

exploring – travelling, discovering new places, learning a language, documentaries

music – listening, playing, composing, dancing, karaoke

socialising – hosting or visiting family or friends, dating, pubs, restaurants

being part of a group – volunteering, religious communities, watching sport with fellow enthusiasts

What do you enjoy?

culture – comedy, films, plays, poetry, museums

creativity – writing, drawing, photography, crafts, or coming up with an idea for a start-up business

being active – team sports, walking, gym, yoga

feeling a sense of achievement – playing computer games, puzzles like Sudoku

It can feel daunting to move to a new place as a student, and challenging to find people with similar interests. Trying university societies is a good first step, as there are probably some like-minded people who meet regularly and enjoy similar things to you.

Rest

How do you rest and relax? Some people are so used to being on the go that they hardly know what it feels like to slow down or stop for a while. Resting or down time is different from the enjoyment of more energised activities described above. Down time is about taking a break from projects and goals. Some people like to reflect on their lives when they relax and others prefer to switch off from their busy minds. One way to take a break from thoughts about the past or future is to focus on the present moment (see Part 2 on mindfulness, p. 29).

THEORY BOX: The Rest Test

In 2016 a large survey of over 18,000 people in 134 countries explored people's subjective experience of rest (Hubbub, 2017). The average amount of rest per day was around 3 hours, and 68% of people said that they would like more rest. People who took 5–6 hours' rest (not including sleep) had significantly higher scores on wellbeing than those who had less than this.

There are no rules for how to rest – it can be alone or with others, it can happen at any time, inside or outside. The main thing is to find some way to allow your body to slow down, to feel content or peaceful, even for a short while.

The top 10 restful activities from the Rest Test are shown below. Which of the activities do you do regularly and which could you include to give yourself more rest?

1 Reading
2 Spending time with nature
3 Being alone
4 Listening to music
5 Doing nothing in particular
6 Walking
7 Having a bath or showering
8 Daydreaming
9 Watching TV
10 Meditating or practising mindfulness

Weekly Planning – Work, Rest and Play

Try to reward yourself after a day of studying by planning pleasurable things to do away from your desk or computer. You could go for a walk, make your favourite meal, listen to music, soak in the bath, watch a film, or phone or meet a friend.

See if you can make plans not just for when and where to work, but also for time off for rest and fun. Do plan in time for fun and rest, even during intense study periods, as otherwise these important activities can get overlooked.

> ### Tips for planning your week
>
> - Plan to do something relaxing each day and an enjoyable activity a couple of times a week.
> - Use a diary or the weekly activity schedule shown below to plan your time.
> - Set realistic goals, and be flexible if you don't achieve each goal.
> - Over time, you will figure out a realistic schedule that works for you.

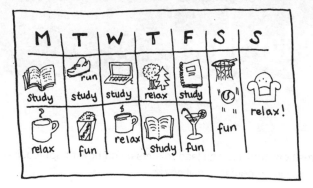

You can bring balance to your life by paying attention to how you sleep, eat, drink and make time for fun and rest. Part 5 offers more ways to manage stress by focusing on how you study.

STUDY SMART

Part 5 explores how studying can lead to stress, and how to approach work in a way that facilitates steady progress. It will cover:

– Studying hard versus studying smart
– Managing procrastination and distractions
– Working with perfectionism
– Managing setbacks.

Studying for a university degree is a little like training for a marathon: both can be physically and mentally tiring, and involve working for several months towards an end result. As well as the training runs, runners need to do stretches, work out in the gym, eat healthy, energy-rich food, get enough sleep, and rest enough to allow their muscles to recover. How does the idea of looking after yourself apply to preparing for exams or a final dissertation? Is it wise to study non-stop for months on end?

Studying hard is something many students feel they ought to do, and are sometimes encouraged to do by others (e.g. family members and tutors). However, this can come with a mind-set that emphasises the hard, but has less of how to study in a smart and efficient way. Let's look at the difference:

Differences between studying hard and studying smart

	Studying hard	Studying smart
Goals	Unrealistic and rigid	Realistic and flexible
Hours per day	Long hours, from early in the morning and late into the night	Manageable hours Your schedule will depend on your other commitments (e.g. paid work, family). See the 'Time Management' Pocket Study Skills Guide, p. 13, for different students' weekly plans.
Time off studying	Little or no time off Feeling self-critical or guilty when not studying	Regular breaks that provide a chance to recharge Doing helpful and enjoyable things during breaks
Long-term consequence	Exhaustion, poor concentration, burnout Less efficient – less knowledge is processed per hour of studying	Stamina to keep studying due to balanced schedule More efficient – better recall and understanding of material

Study breaks

Stay focused by giving your brain regular, short breaks. It is easier to concentrate, knowing that you have a break coming up. The Pomodoro Time Management Technique® recommends studying for blocks of around 25 minutes followed by a 5-minute break, particularly if you are finding it hard to concentrate (Cirillo Consulting, 2016).[1]

Some students develop back, shoulder, neck, and wrist problems from sitting and writing or typing for long periods at a time. To prevent becoming stiff and achy, try the following stretches during your study breaks: www.300hours.com/articles/11-exercise-stretches-to-break-up-the-study-monotony (300 hours, 2017).

Of course, your concentration will depend on the task: if you are fully engaged in something, you may be able to concentrate for much longer than 25 minutes. After three or four rounds of 25-minute study blocks, take a longer break, for at least 30 minutes.

---

[1]The Pomodoro Technique® is a registered trademark by Francesco Cirillo. This book is not affiliated with, associated with, or endorsed by the Pomodoro Technique® or Francesco Cirillo.

Do you study hard, or study smart? It may feel scary to switch to studying smart, if you've been used to studying hard for some time. Why not try an experiment of alternating between these approaches (i.e. one day 'studying hard', one day 'studying smart')? Afterwards, compare the impact on your stress levels and productivity.

There are more tips on planning your week in the 'Time Management' Pocket Study Skills Guide, p. 12.

16 Managing procrastination and distractions

Procrastination

Procrastination is one of the most common reasons that prevent students from studying smart. It involves putting off doing a task that could be done sooner, and can involve:

- Prioritising less important tasks over more important ones
- Prioritising pleasurable activities over less pleasurable ones
- Making excuses as to why something else should take priority over work.

There are many reasons why we procrastinate. One way to understand this is to imagine how you would feel if you couldn't procrastinate on a task. Often people who procrastinate say: '*I'd feel anxious and agitated*', '*I'd feel bored*' and '*I'd feel like I wouldn't know how to do the work*'. As you can see, in these examples procrastination is a way of avoiding unpleasant feelings. Whilst this is understandable, over an extended period, procrastination can lead to increased stress levels, anxiety and increased illness symptoms as a deadline approaches (Tice and Baumeister, 1997).

Here are five steps you can take to help if you are struggling with procrastination:

1 Notice when you procrastinate (i.e. if you're doing tasks that aren't important, or keep on checking social media or watching TV when part of you knows there's work to be done).

2 Try to recognise the function of the procrastination – the reason why you are switching task (e.g. to avoid unpleasant feelings like anxiety, or a concern that you don't know how to complete the work or might fail it).

3 Spend time practising mindfulness (p. 29) or imagery (p. 47) as a way to help you manage this struggle.

4 Take a moment to refocus on the original task – start with using the Pomodoro Technique® of working on it for 25 minutes, followed by a short break.

5 Try not to beat yourself up if you find this difficult or don't succeed the first time – it takes practice to change a habit (see the 'Time Management' Pocket Study Skills Guide, p. 88, for more tips on addressing procrastination).

Distraction

Distractions are a common way to procrastinate. Distracting activities come in many forms: from re-organising files and cleaning the bathroom, to becoming intrigued by topics unrelated to work! A major distraction for many students involves technology – mobile phones, tablets, laptops and box sets.

Switch off

It is important to switch off, literally! Many of us are becoming increasingly reliant on smartphones, tablets and computers for studying, communicating, and entertainment – so much so that in some cases, these are like extensions of our bodies! A 2016 study found that adults check their phone on average 46 times a day. For 18 to 24-year-olds, the average was 74 times per day. Other studies have estimated that people check their phones every 6 minutes, which can be up to 150 times a day (Deloitte, 2017).

How often do you check your phone or computer and how does it affect you? If you are not sure whether you are becoming reliant on technology, ask yourself the following questions (Colier, 2016):

– Do you feel anxious if you can't check for messages (e.g. if you lose your phone or have no reception)?
– Do you keep using technology when you know it is causing problems in other areas of your life (e.g. studying, relationships)?
– Have you given up activities that you used to enjoy (e.g. reading novels for pleasure; playing sports) in order to use technology?

If you answered yes to at least two of these questions, technology may be impacting on your quality of life and it is worth trying to cut down your use.

In an experiment, 136 people were asked to do a cognitive task. There were three groups:

1. people who did the task with no distractions
2. people who were distracted by an electronic message
3. people who were expecting a message that did not arrive.

The second group, who were distracted by a message, performed 20% worse than the first group, who were not distracted. Interestingly, the third group, who were on alert but did not actually receive a message, also performed 20% worse than the first group (Sullivan and Thompson, 2013).

So, when people know that they may receive a message, their concentration suffers. In other words, turning off all messaging devices while studying could significantly improve your academic performance!

Using smartphones excessively can also contribute to stress. A study of over 300 university students found that students who used their smartphones more frequently were more likely to experience stress, frustration, and social anxiety (Lee et al., 2014).

Looking at phones or computers late at night can make it harder to get to sleep (Khazan, 2015). This is because the screen light tricks the brain into thinking that it is still daytime by suppressing the release of a sleep hormone, melatonin.

Tips for switching off your phone

- Leave your phone on silent out of arm's reach when you are studying or going to sleep. The physical distance will reduce your temptation to check it.
- Try a weekly 'digital detox' to give yourself a couple of hours' break from screens. Go for a walk without your phone, and experience tranquillity with no interruptions!
- Bear in mind that switching off may feel uncomfortable, or even anxiety provoking, at first.

How to switch off distracting websites

If you are working on a computer, only open the programs that are strictly relevant to your current work. If you tend to become distracted by email and social media websites, you can install a program that blocks distracting websites for set periods of time. All of these work on PC and Mac systems.

Focus-boosting study apps

Programme	Description
Focus booster	Plans your time to focus on a task for 25 minutes then take a 5-minute break www.focusboosterapp.com
Freedom	Blocks out distracting websites for a set time https://freedom.to
Stay Focusd	Rather than blocking sites, this app allows you a set period of time on distracting websites a day www.stayfocusd.com

Programme	Description
Focus writer	Creates a distraction-free screen to improve focus on writing (e.g. no menus or clock). You can set daily goals for writing too. https://gottcode.org/focuswriter

(adapted from http://99u.com/articles/6969/10-online-tools-for-better-attention-focus)

Do you set consistently high standards that are tough to meet? When you meet a standard, do you set a higher goal for yourself? Do you criticise yourself when you don't meet your standards? Do you expect more of yourself than you expect of others? If you nodded to some of these questions, you may have perfectionist tendencies.

Perfectionism is tricky to address, since it can drive people to work hard and succeed. A common worry is that by becoming less perfectionist, performance will slip, and results will suffer. So, it is vital to consider whether perfectionism is working for you or against you. The following examples of two final-year students, Rima and Jake, illustrate the difference between when high standards are motivating and when they are demoralising.

Rima and Jake were in the same History class, working towards their final-year dissertation. Both were keen to get a high mark, and saw academic success as important to their self-esteem and future career. Rima read several books and articles, made some notes, and started writing early. When she got stressed, she called a friend for advice and support. Jake thought that he needed to read everything on the

subject before he could start writing. He became overwhelmed with all the material he had gathered and only had two days to write up. Due to the time pressure, he became stressed, panicky and found it hard to concentrate. He had to stay up all night to finish the dissertation. Who do you think did a better dissertation? And how do you think they both felt by the end?

Although both Rima and Jake have very high standards, they have different approaches to studying. Whereas Rima has a healthy desire to do well, which allows her to stay productive by pacing herself, Jake's rigid form of perfectionism slowed him down, caused a great deal of stress and ultimately stopped him from writing a good piece of work.

Given that perfectionism can lead to stress and poor concentration, here are some ideas on how to keep it in check.

Keeping perfectionism in check

To keep perfectionist traits in check so that you feel motivated rather than overwhelmed, two approaches can help: learning when to apply the high standards and seeing the bigger picture.

Learning when to apply high standards

Think back to the marathon runners 'Train hard' and 'Train smart' on p. 73. Since marathon runners need to pace themselves, they choose when to conserve their energy and when to push themselves to run faster. The same idea of pacing yourself applies to studies. Sometimes it is worth applying high standards (e.g. writing a strong conclusion in a final dissertation) and at other times it is not necessary (e.g. re-writing revision notes so that they are super neat), or even detrimental (e.g. doing further research when you have already collected too much material and the deadline is looming).

See if you can pace yourself by applying high standards when they matter, rather than across the board.

Seeing the bigger picture

You can also tackle unhealthy perfectionism by seeing the bigger picture and considering how you value yourself as a person. Do you judge yourself solely on your achievements and grades? Many students evaluate themselves on their achievements, as grades are easily measurable. Although your studies are important, you are not defined by just your grades. There are other aspects to life such as family, friends, interests, exercise, wellbeing, and community. Think about these questions:

- How important is your family to you?
- How much do you value friendships and relationships?
- What do you enjoy outside of studying (music, reading, sport, hobbies, going out)?
- How do you look after yourself (eating well, exercise, relaxation)?
- Do you think about the bigger picture? Are you a member of a community or interested in wider causes (politics, religion, human rights, volunteering, the environment)?

Being a student is only one role and you have a range of other roles to play.

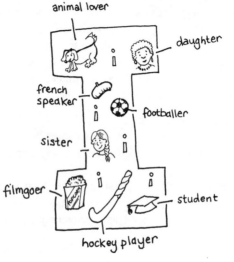

This diagram shows that we do not just have one identity (one 'big I') as we are all made up of many identities and roles ('little i's) that change and develop over time.

Coping with feedback

Your approach to studying will affect how you respond to feedback. If you get critical feedback on a piece of work (which is likely to happen at some point), it is natural to feel disappointed.

Reflect How do you respond to feedback? Could you respond in a more constructive way?

Tips for receiving feedback on your work

▶ View comments as specific to the assignment, rather than a judgement on you as a person.

▶ Use comments constructively to plan what you can change or improve.

▶ Ask your tutor or adviser for clarification if there is anything you don't understand or if you don't know how to improve your work.

▶ Remember that other people's comments can be subjective (e.g. even though one tutor does not like your writing style, another might). After all, 12 publishers rejected JK Rowling before one recognised how good her book was!

▶ Try not to beat yourself up if you get negative feedback. Instead, try to treat yourself in an encouraging and supportive way, similar to how you might do for a friend who's experienced a setback or negative comments.

Asking for help is not a weakness – successful people across the world have relied upon the support and feedback of others to help them get to where they are.

Problems arise when students become distressed and demotivated by critical comments, or feel that the criticism is an indication of a serious flaw in themselves. This can lead to a loss of confidence, rumination on the perceived failure, and difficulties in moving on.

Although it is not always easy, the most constructive way forward is to take on board the feedback so that you can improve your work and move forwards.

Achievement mindset versus learning mindset

There are different ways to approach studying at university. Let's look at this with a short quiz.

QUIZ: Your studying mindset

Consider how important the following statements are to you. Rate each one on a scale of 1 to 10:

1	2	3	4	5	6	7	8	9	10

Not at all important   Extremely important

How important is it for you to:

1 develop a sound knowledge of your subject and related areas?
2 get good grades or come top of your class?
3 find your lectures stimulating or personally meaningful?
4 do well in a module, regardless of whether you enjoy it?

Your approach to studying will have a major impact on your ability to cope with
challenges at university. Students with a purely achievement-driven mindset simply
want to achieve top marks. Whilst this is understandable, it tends to lead to stress
because their self-esteem is contingent upon being successful and getting top
grades. And what happens if you don't get the top grade?

In comparison, students with a learning-driven mindset want to learn and grow
over time. They, too, want to do well in their studies and essays, but they don't
evaluate themselves solely on academic success. Students with a learning mindset
are engaged in their studies because they are personally meaningful or stimulating,
rather than because they lead to a particular grade or outcome. Successful students

are more likely to adopt a learning-driven mindset. This is because learning from all types of experiences – success, failure, and everything in between – leads to better recovery from setbacks, and a lower likelihood of giving up when studying becomes tough (Mangels et al., 2006).

In reality, most students are likely to adopt a combination of both mindsets. There are times when an achievement mindset is more likely to play a role (e.g. final exams, getting a job). However, it is worth remembering that studying is not just about achieving; it is also about learning and making progress.

Focus on the journey, not the destination

Coping with setbacks

Sometimes life gets in the way of studying. Setbacks can be particularly hard for students struggling with perfectionism, as anything unexpected that gets in the way of their end goal can lead them to feel stressed and upset. Even if you prepare well in advance and devise a comprehensive revision timetable, things don't always work out as planned.

Setbacks can be related to studying, such as:

- your computer breaking down
- a lab experiment taking longer than expected
- waiting for research ethics approval
- a lecturer or supervisor moving to another university.

They can also relate to your personal life, for instance:

- losing your part-time job or grant
- problems with your landlord
- becoming unwell or having an accident
- a break-up, or a relationship ending
- bereavement or family illness.

Tips for coping with setbacks

▸ Be supportive and flexible with yourself if you need to take a break from studying.
▸ Be open with your tutor or adviser about situations affecting your studies, sooner rather than later.
▸ Although some tutors are better than others at talking about personal issues, your university has a duty to take your situation into account.
▸ Remember that your tutors and professors were students once, so they have probably experienced some challenges along the way.
▸ You may need to apply for extenuating circumstances to be considered, and provide evidence of how your studies have been affected – you can speak to someone in the student support or university counselling centre about this.

It is natural to be disappointed if you have a setback; see if you can speak to a friend, or if there's something that you can learn that will be helpful for the future.

Conclusion

This guide has covered what stress is, when it is triggered at university, and how it affects the mind and body. Although stress is a natural human experience that arises in response to pressure, it can become overwhelming if you don't notice the signs and take steps to manage it. The good news is that there are many ways to manage stress, so that you can keep studying and enjoying life at university.

If you find that the ideas and tips in this book have not helped and you feel unable to manage stress or anxiety, it may be worth talking to a professional (see Ideas for Further Support, p. 98).

Final Take-Away Points:

➣ University is a time of transition – the numerous changes to your academic, personal and social life can feel exciting, but also stressful.

➣ Stress can be triggered both externally (e.g. by conflicts or time pressure) and internally (e.g. by worries and ruminating).

➣ You can develop a different relationship with stress so that it becomes manageable (e.g. by noticing the loops in your mind and stepping away from them).

- It is worth paying attention to your emotions, as they tend to signal that something needs to change.
- Making the most out of university and keeping stress in check is about striking a balance between studying, resting, and enjoying yourself.
- Studying smart and focusing on learning rather than achievement are two approaches that will help you to make progress in your studies and minimise stress.

Although the examples in this book are tailored to undergraduate and postgraduate students, the ideas should also prove useful for life after university. The world of work brings with it not only situations that are similar to those at university (e.g. meeting colleagues for the first time, being appraised), but also novel challenges (e.g. job interviews, adjusting to a new working schedule, meeting targets). Your post-university life may involve juggling other responsibilities, such as repaying loans or looking after family members. Although transitions on leaving university can feel challenging and exciting, they can also trigger stress in some shape or form.

Hopefully, the life skills of looking after your mind (e.g. noticing stress loops, practising mindfulness) and looking after your body (e.g. developing a work–life balance by getting enough sleep and taking regular breaks) are now in your toolbox to help you manage stress in the years to come.

Crisis support

If you feel in need of urgent support or are in crisis

– Go to your local hospital Accident & Emergency department.
– See your GP (local doctor).
– Samaritans offer a 24-hour telephone and email support service for people in the UK:
  Tel. – 116 123   Email – jo@samaritans.org   Website – www.samaritans.org

Help at your university

– You can seek support at your university support centre or university counselling centre. They may refer you to other services, such as the Careers Service or Accommodation service if there are specific practical issues to address.
– If you need academic support, you can also see your tutor or adviser.
– Nightline is a student-run telephone helpline that runs in UK universities during term-time.
  To find your local Nightline service, see: www.nightline.ac.uk/want-to-talk

Further counselling or therapy

If you want more psychological support than your university or local NHS service can offer, you can look into private therapy. If possible, it is worth getting a recommendation for a therapist. There may be low-cost options in your local area so it is worth asking your GP or researching online.

Here are two national organisations where you can find an accredited therapist.

Cognitive Behavioural Therapy

CBT is a short-to-medium-term, evidence-based treatment that tends to focus on how to break current patterns that are affecting your life. You can find an accredited CBT therapist here:

www.cbtregisteruk.com/Default.aspx

Counselling and Psychodynamic Therapy

Counselling offers a confidential, supportive space to discuss emotional issues and difficult life situations. Psychodynamic therapy is usually a longer-term therapy that focuses on how patterns have developed based on experiences growing up. You can find an accredited counsellor or psychotherapist here:

www.itsgoodtotalk.org.uk/therapists

References

300 hours (2017) 11 exercise stretches to break up study monotony. Available at: www.300hours.com/articles/11-exercise-stretches-to-break-up-the-study-monotony

American Psychological Association (2017) Stress effects on the body. Available at: www.apa.org/helpcenter/stress-body.aspx

Chee M W L and Chuah L Y M (2008) Functional neuroimaging insights into how sleep and sleep deprivation affect memory and cognition. *Current Opinion in Neurology*, **21** (4), pp. 417–423.

Cirillo Consulting GMBH (2011–2016) Pomodoro Time Management Technique®. Available at: https://cirillocompany.de/pages/pomodoro-technique

Colier N (2016) *The power of off: The mindful way to stay sane in a virtual world.* Boulder, CO: Sounds True.

Deloitte (2017) 2016 global mobile consumer survey: US edition. Available at: www2.deloitte.com/us/en/pages/technology-media-and-telecommunications/articles/global-mobile-consumer-survey-us-edition.html

Gilbert P (2009) *The compassionate mind*. London: Constable.

Gillen-O'Neel C, Huynh V W and Fuligni A J (2013) Sleep or studying – the academic costs of extra studying at the expense of sleep. *Child Development*, **84** (10), pp. 133–142.

Godman H (2014) Regular exercise changes the brain to improve memory, thinking skills. Harvard health publications. Available at: www.health.harvard.edu/blog/regular-exercise-changes-brain-improve-memory-thinking-skills-201404097110

Hershner S D and Chervin R D (2014) Causes and consequences of sleepiness in college students. *Nature and Science of Sleep*, **6**, pp. 73–84.

Hubbub (2017) The Rest Test: A Hubbub collaboration with Radio 4. Available at: http://hubbubresearch.org/rest-test-results

Irons C and Beaumont E (2017) *The compassionate mind workbook: A step-by-step guide to developing your compassionate self*. London: Little, Brown.

Khazan O (2015) How smartphones hurt sleep. Available at: www.theatlantic.com/health/archive/2015/02/how-smartphones-are-ruining-our-sleep/ 385792

Lee R (2013) Chronic dehydration more common than you think. CBS Miami. Available at: http://miami.cbslocal.com/2013/07/02/chronic-dehydration-more-common-than-you-think

Lee Y K, Chang C T, Lin Y and Cheng Z H (2014) The dark side of smartphone usage: Psychological traits, compulsive behavior and technostress. *Computers and Human Behaviour*, **31**, pp. 373–383.

Mangels J A, Butterfield B, Lamb J, Good C and Dweck C S (2006) Why do beliefs about intelligence influence learning success? Learning goals better than performance goals? A social-cognitive-neuroscience model. *Social, Cognitive, and Affective Neuroscience*, **1** (2), pp. 75–86.

McGonigal K (2015) *The upside of stress: Why stress is good for you (and how to get good at It)*. London: Vermilion.

NHS (2015) Risk of alcohol misuse. Available at: www.nhs.uk/Conditions/Alcohol-misuse/Pages/Risks.aspx

NHS (2016) Exercise for depression. Available at: www.nhs.uk/Conditions/stress-anxiety-depression/Pages/Exercise-for-depression.aspx

National Institutes of Health (2017) How much sleep is enough? Available at: www.nhlbi.nih.gov/health/health-topics/topics/sdd/howmuch

National Sleep Foundation (2017) What is good quality sleep? Available at: https://sleepfoundation.org/press-release/what-good-quality-sleep

Park C L, Armeli S and Howard T (2004) The daily stress and coping process and alcohol use among college students. *Journal of Studies on Alcohol*, **65**, pp. 126–135.

Points Sports Health (2017) Hit the gym before you hit the books. Available at: www.pointssports.com/the-benefits-of-exercise-for-studying

Public Health England (2016) The Eatwell Guide. Available at: www.nhs.uk/Livewell/Goodfood/Pages/the-eatwell-guide.aspx

Sominsky L and Spencer S J (2014) Eating behavior and stress: A pathway to obesity. *Frontiers in Psychology*, **5**, pp. 434–438.

Sullivan B and Thompson H (2013) Brain, interrupted. Available at: www.nytimes.com/2013/05/05/opinion/sunday/a-focus-on-distraction.html

Tice D M and Baumeister R F (1997) Longitudinal study of procrastination, performance, stress and health: The costs and benefits of dawdling. *Psychological Science*, **8** (6), pp. 454–458.

Verster J C, Alford C, Bervoets A C, de Klerk S, Grange J A, Hogewoning A, Jones K, Kruisselbrink D L, Owen L, Piasecki T M, Raasveld S J, Royle S, Slutske W S, Smith G S, Stephens R and the Alcohol Hangover Research Group (2013) Hangover research needs: Proceedings of the 5th Alcohol Hangover Research Group Meeting. *Current Drug Abuse Review*, **6** (3), pp. 245–251.

Yerkes R M and Dodson J D (1908) The relation of strength of stimulus to rapidity of habit-formation. *Journal of Comparative Neurology and Psychology*, **18**, pp. 459–482.

Useful sources

Evidence for the benefits of mindfulness

Davidson R J et al. (2003) Alterations in brain and immune function produced by mindfulness meditation. *Psychosomatic Medicine*, **65** (4): 564–570.

Hutcherson C et al. (2008) Loving-kindness: Meditation increases social connectedness. *Emotion*, **8** (5), pp. 720–724.

Querstret D, Cropley M and Fife-Schaw C (2017) Internet-based instructor-led mindfulness for work-related rumination, fatigue, and sleep: Assessing facets of mindfulness as mechanisms of change. A randomized waitlist control trial. *Journal of Occupational Health Psychology*, **22** (2), pp. 153–169.

Tang Y et al. (2007) Short-term meditation training improves attention and self-regulation. *Proceedings of the National Academy of Sciences for United States of America*, **104** (43), 17152–17156.

Teasdale J et al. (2000) Prevention of relapse/recurrence in major depression by mindfulness-based cognitive therapy. *Journal of Counselling and Clinical Psychology*, **68** (4), pp. 615–623.

Websites for further reading

The Compassionate Mind Foundation offers articles, videos and downloadable meditations from Compassion Focused Therapy. Available at: https://compassionate-mind.co.uk

Cognitive Behavioural Therapy self-help resources and workbooks on a wide range of issues including stress, anxiety, low mood, perfectionism and low self-esteem are available free from: www.getselfhelp.co.uk and www.cci.health.wa.gov.au

Mindfulness for Students provides links to mindfulness resources and audio tracks, available at: http://mindfulnessforstudents.co.uk

Students against depression provides resources for students with stress, low mood, available at: http://studentsagainstdepression.org

Apps for computers or smart phones

7-minute workout – a full body workout you can do with no equipment that includes 12 exercises and takes just 7 minutes. For options, see www.guidingtech.com/27928/best-free-7-minute-workout-apps/

Breathing Zone – guided breathing which allows you to set your own time frame for mindfulness, available at: www.breathing.zone

Headspace – mindfulness app with a free trial and animations to explain mindfulness. Available at: www.headspace.com

Index